Contents

Page

Weblink: www.curriculumvisions.com

Plants and animals

Animals and plants need each other.

Daisies.

Plants grow in the ground. They have roots, leaves, stems and flowers.

Flowers in the garden, wild flowers, trees and bushes are all plants. Trees and bushes are plants with woody trunks and branches.

Plants are food for animals.

A woodland of beech trees.

Animals move around. Many animals, such as slugs and ants, eat plants for food. Animals, such as birds, help plants to scatter their seeds. They also use trees and other plants to nest in.

ants

Ospreys in their nest high in a tree.

A slug eats leaves for its food.

Ants run up grass stems, looking for food.

How can you tell a plant from an animal?

Life in a park

A park is a mixture of wildlife and things we have grown.

Most of the ground in a park is covered in grass.

In places there are bushes, flower beds and also many different trees. These are often grouped together.

There are large areas of grass in a park.

It's easy to see lots of different flowers in a park.

Butterflies move from flower to flower.

Spiders weave their webs in the bushes.

Woodlice live under rotting branches.

Most of the wildlife in a park is small. Many of the animals are insects such as ants and butterflies. There will be some larger animals such as squirrels and birds, and there may be ducks on a pond.

Larger animals, such as foxes, come out at night when there are no people about.

Which are easier to see in a park – plants or animals?

Weblink: www.curriculumvisions.com

Under a tree

A tree casts a shadow and keeps out the light – and most plants.

Trees are the biggest plants. They grow lots of leaves and spread them out to catch the light. The leaves make it shady under the tree. It is too dim for most other plants to grow.

The tree also takes up water with its roots. This makes the soil too dry for other plants.

It is shady and dry under a tree.

Weblink: www.curriculumvisions.com

Few animals live under a tree. You may see a few beetles crawling around on the ground and earthworms may pull dead leaves down into the soil.

beetle

earthworms

Why are there few plants under the trees?

Weblink: www.curriculumvisions.com

The pond

Ponds have water all year round, so this is where water-loving plants and animals live.

Some plants, such as water lilies and waterweed, grow in deep water. Other plants, such as rushes, grow with their roots in shallow water and send their leaves and flowers above the water.

bullrush

duckweed

water lily

Many kinds of plant grow in a pond.

10

Many animals live near a pond. In the pond there are fish, insects and tadpoles. On the surface there are insects such as pond skaters. Dragonflies fly about over the water. Herons look for food in the pond.

A heron waits for a fish to swim near.

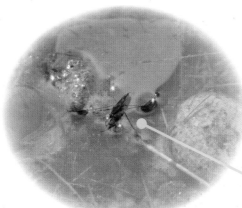

A pond skater lives on the water surface.

pond skater

Fish swim under water lily pads (leaves).

A dragonfly rests on a plant.

A pond snail crawls over waterweed.

Can you name some common pond animals?

Weblink: www.curriculumvisions.com

The rock pool

Rock pools at the seaside are different from ponds. They are full of salty sea water.

sea anemones

starfish

Many plants and animals live close together in the clear water of a rock pool.

Rock pools are full of salty water. The water changes twice a day as the tide comes in and out.

The most common plant in a rock pool is seaweed. It can be green, red or brown.

Animals, such as shrimps, crabs and starfish move about. You may see limpets and sea anemones, too.

Many birds hunt in the rock pools. Seagulls are common visitors.

Starfish are slow-moving animals. They have a mouth on their undersides.

Crabs scuttle about, keeping out of sight of birds.

Shrimps make jerking movements close to the bottom of the pool.

Periwinkles and other 'sea-snails' crawl around on the rock pool sides.

How are rock pools different from ponds?

Weblink: www.curriculumvisions.com

How seeds are made

Seeds are made in flowers.

Inside each flower is a dust called pollen.
This is important for making seeds.

When pollen from one plant reaches another plant,
the flower changes and starts to make seeds.

In time, the petals fall away and the seeds grow.

1 Bees and the wind carry the pollen from flower to flower. This bee is on a dandelion.

Weblink: www.curriculumvisions.com

2 The petals fall off the flower and the seeds grow. In the case of a dandelion the seeds have white tufts on their ends.

3 The seeds can be carried away by the wind or by animals.

seeds

How do bees help flowers?

15

7 Seeds, fruits and nuts

Flowers make seeds in all shapes and sizes. They can be found in fruit and nuts.

Flowers make seeds. In most flowers the seeds form in a soft fruit. In a few flowers the seed forms in a hard woody case called a nut.

Some flowers, like grass, make small dry fruits. Their seeds are called grains. Others, like the sycamore, make larger seeds or fruits.

Wheat is a kind of grass. We eat its grains.

sycamore wings

The sycamore fruit has a wing which helps the seed move through the air as it falls.

The acorn is a nut with one seed inside. It forms from the flowers of the oak tree.

Weblink: www.curriculumvisions.com

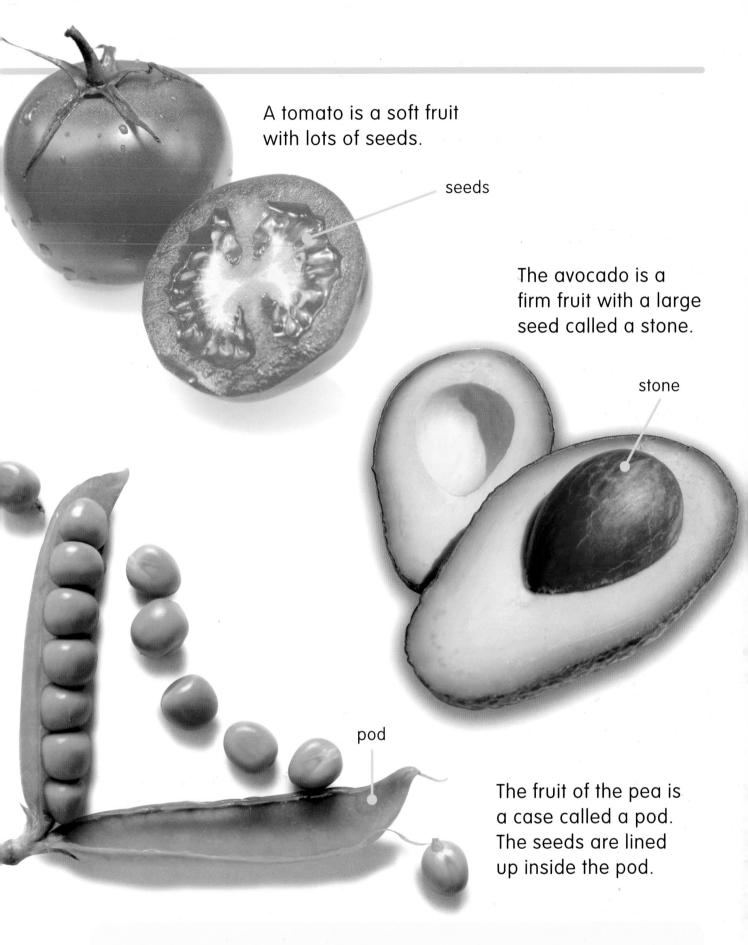

A tomato is a soft fruit with lots of seeds.

seeds

The avocado is a firm fruit with a large seed called a stone.

stone

pod

The fruit of the pea is a case called a pod. The seeds are lined up inside the pod.

Where are the seeds in an orange and an apple?

Weblink: www.curriculumvisions.com

Sprouting seeds

A seed will begin to make a new plant when it has water and warmth. The plant will only grow if it has water, warmth and light.

1 When a seed is in moist, warm soil it begins to swell. The root comes out of the seed first. It finds more water to keep the seed sprouting.

2 After the root has pushed down into the soil it can suck up water. Now is the time for the plant to send up a stem and the first two leaves.

When do you think the plant begins to make flowers?

3 The leaves turn green in the light. The leaves make food that helps the plant to grow. Pairs of leaves appear as the shoot gets taller. The flowers appear last of all.

A butterfly

Some animals change a lot as they grow up. Butterflies are a good example.

Butterflies are grown-up insects, but they don't start with wings. They start as caterpillars. When a butterfly egg hatches, a soft-bodied caterpillar climbs out. The caterpillar has many legs and no wings.

As the caterpillar eats leaves, it grows fatter and bigger. Later, it goes to sleep and changes into a butterfly.

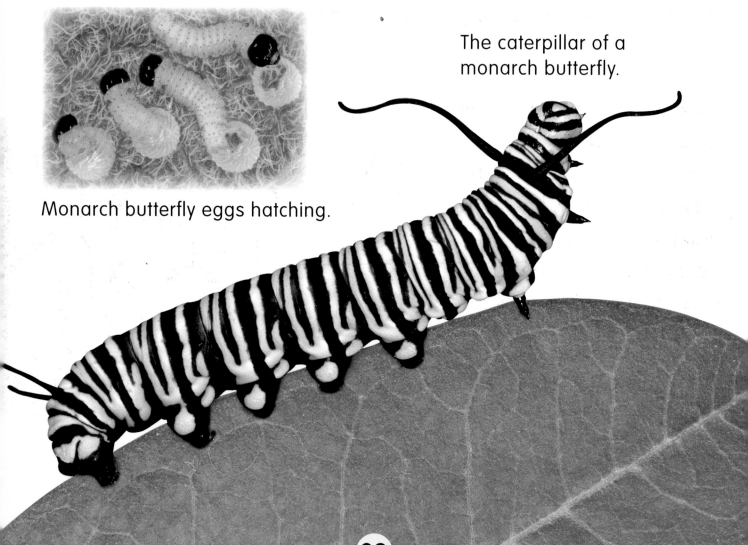

The caterpillar of a monarch butterfly.

Monarch butterfly eggs hatching.

chrysalis

Here is the caterpillar making a 'sleeping bag' or chrysalis.

Here is the monarch butterfly.

When it has grown as much as it can, the caterpillar stops eating. It fastens itself to a twig and then begins to make a silky coat. This coat hardens around the caterpillar. It is called a chrysalis.

In time, the chrysalis breaks open and a butterfly comes out.

How is the caterpillar different from the butterfly?

Words to learn

Flower bed

A piece of ground where flowers are grown.

Heron

A bird with long legs that wades in water and eats fish and frogs.

Insect

An animal with six legs.

Osprey

A large bird which eats fish.

Pond skater

An insect with long legs that lives on the surface of a pond.

Weblink: www.curriculumvisions.com

Sea anemone

A jellyfish which sticks to a rock.

Sea snail

An animal that has a shell like a snail but lives in the sea.

Spider

An animal with eight legs.

Wildlife

All the animals living in an outdoor place, such as a garden, park or wood.

Woodlice

Small grey animals with fourteen legs.

Weblink: www.curriculumvisions.com

Index

CurriculumVisions 2B Science@School

Plants and animals

Brian Knapp

Curriculum Visions

Science@School

Teacher's Guide
There is a Teacher's Guide available to accompany this book.

Dedicated Web Site
There is a wealth of supporting material including videos and activities available at the Professional Zone, part of our dedicated web site:

www.CurriculumVisions.com

The Professional Zone
is a subscription zone.

A CVP Book.
First published in 2008

Copyright © 2008 Earthscape

The rights of Peter Riley and Brian Knapp to be identified as the authors of this work have been asserted by them in accordance with the Copyright, Designs and Patents Act 1988.

All rights reserved. No part of this publication may be reproduced, stored in a retrieval system, or transmitted in any form or by any means, electronic, mechanical, photocopying, recording or otherwise, without prior permission of the publisher and the copyright holder.

Authors
Peter Riley, BSc, C Biol, MI Biol, PGCE, and Brian Knapp, BSc, PhD

Senior Designer
Adele Humphries, BA, PGCE

Educational Consultant
Jan Smith (former Deputy Head of Wellfield School, Burnley, Lancashire)

Editor
Gillian Gatehouse

Designed and produced by
EARTHSCAPE

Printed in China by
WKT Co., Ltd

Curriculum Visions Science@School
Volume 2B Plants and animals
A CIP record for this book is available from the British Library.
ISBN: 978 1 86214 260 2

Picture credits
All pictures are from the Earthscape and ShutterStock collections.

This product is manufactured from sustainable managed forests. For every tree cut down at least one more is planted.

Ants are insects. Insects are animals.